DISCOVER AND DO!

PLANTS

Written by Jane Lacey

Enslow PUBLISHING

Published in 2023 by Enslow Publishing, LLC
29 East 21st Street, New York, NY 10010

Editor: Katie Dicker
Designer: Clare Nicholas
Series Designer: Rocket Design (East Anglia) Ltd

Manufactured in the United States of America

CPSIA compliance information: Batch #CSENS23: For further information contact
Enslow Publishing LLC, New York, New York at 1-800-398-2504.

Please visit our website, www.enslowpublishing.com. For a free color catalog of all our high-quality books,
call toll free 1-800-398-2504 or fax 1-877-980-4454.

Cataloging-in-Publication Data

Names: Lacey, Jane.

Title: Plants / Jane Lacey.

Description: New York : Enslow Publishing, 2023. | Series: Discover and do! | Includes glossary and index.

Identifiers: ISBN 9781978530744 (pbk.) | ISBN 9781978530768 (library bound) | ISBN 9781978530751 (6pack) | ISBN 9781978530775 (ebook)

Subjects: LCSH: Plants--Juvenile literature.

Classification: LCC QK49.L334 2023 | DDC 581--dc23

Picture credits:

t=top b=bottom m=middle l=left r=right

Shutterstock: BlueRingMedia cover/title page r, 5tl, 7bl, 14t, 18b and 30bl, Mushakesa 4, 20b and 30tr, Belii_medved 5tr and 9tr, bulatova 5br and 16tl, SaveJungle 6b, cobalt88 7tr and 31b, Kalashnikov Dmitry 7bm, Nikitina Olga 8t, Vadym Nechyporenko 8bm, Incomible 10l, lukpedclub 10m and 29br, Kumer Oksana 16tr, Bohdana Seheda 16b, Bur_malin 16, Kazakova Maryia 18tr, Colorcocktail 18tl and 27, insima 20tr and 29tr, Midorie 20t, Cultura Motion 21mr, November_Seventeen 22t, Denys Bogdanov 23tr and 32, Rhoeo 24t, Cute vector illustration 24t, Ihor Bulyhin 24t, Merggy 24b, tetiana_u 24b, Hennadii H 24b and 28bl, Elena Schweitzer 25t, Thyrymn2 25m, Joellen L Armstrong 25b, Neokryuger 27, Inspiring 27, Abscent 27, Alex Oakenman 27; Getty: Macrovector cover/title page l, Aleksandr Durnov 8b, BrianAJackson 12t, andegro4ka 12b, kbeis 14b, energy 21ml, Toltemara 22b, Nicole S. Young 25bl, ikryannikovgmailcom 26t and 31t, amathers 26b.

All design elements from Shutterstock.

Craft models from a previous series by Q2AMedia.

DISCOVER AND DO!

PLANTS

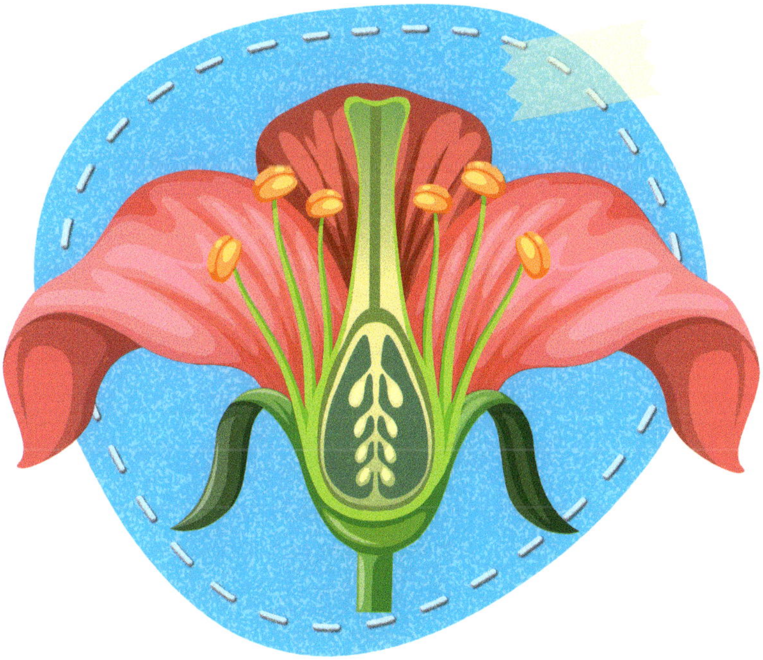

Written by Jane Lacey

Enslow PUBLISHING

CONTENTS

Words that appear in **bold** can be found in the glossary on pages 28–29.

WHAT IS A PLANT?

Plants are alive. Like all living things, they need food and water to live and grow. But unlike other living things, they make their own food. Plants use air, water, and a green pigment in their leaves called chlorophyll to make food from sunlight.

Plants for life

Plants grow all over planet Earth. Life on Earth couldn't exist without plants. They provide food for animals and people. They help to keep the air full of the **oxygen** we breathe. Plants are also part of the **water cycle** because they absorb, or take in, water and release it into the air as a gas called **water vapor**.

Flowering plants

Most plants are flowering plants. The flower is the part of the plant where **fruit** and **seeds** are made. New plants grow from the seeds. Flowering plants are all shapes and sizes. A big horse chestnut tree is a type of flowering plant, and so is a tiny daisy and a prickly cactus.

New sunflower plants grow from seeds that fall from the center of a sunflower.

Non-flowering plants

Plants that don't produce flowers are called non-flowering plants. They make new plants from **spores** instead of seeds. Moss is a non-flowering plant that grows on logs and walls. Its spores look like tiny specks of dust.

Ferns are a type of non-flowering plant. The brown clusters on this fern hold its spores.

Seaweed is a type of non-flowering plant that grows in sea water.

PARTS OF A PLANT

Flowering plants all have roots, a stem, leaves, and flowers. Roots take in water and hold the plant in place, the stem supports the plant, green leaves make food for the plant, and the flower is where seeds are formed.

All parts of a plant need to be healthy for it to grow well.

Drinking in water

Water and **minerals** from the soil are sucked up through the plant's roots and carried along tubes in the roots, stem, and leaves. The veins you see on leaves carry this water and food. Roots and leaves have a skin that keeps in water. Some water vapor escapes through tiny holes in the leaves.

Different plants

Plants **adapt** to survive where they live. Daisies have thin, fine roots that hold the plants in place in shallow soil. Trees have a woody stem to hold them upright. Ivy stems bend and curl up walls, fences, and other plants for support.

All these different plants have roots, stems, leaves, and flowers.

ACTIVITY

WATCH WATER GO THROUGH A PLANT

You will need:

- **3 jars of water**
- **blue food coloring**
- **old carrot**
- **celery stalk with leaves**
- **white carnation**
- **paper and crayons (or a camera)**

1. Put enough drops of food coloring in each jar to make the water a strong blue color.

2. Put the carrot, the celery stalk and the carnation in the jars.

3. Draw the plant in each jar, copying the colors as accurately as you can (or take a picture).

4. Look at the jars every few hours during the day and again the next day. Draw or take a picture of the changes you see. Record your findings on a chart.

Does the carrot, the celery, or the flower look the most blue at the end of your experiment? How quickly do the changes occur? Why do you think this is?

	Carrot (root)	**Celery (stalk and leaves)**	**Carnation (flower)**	**Comments**
2 hours		blue lines starting to show at the bottom of the celery stalk		
8 hours				
24 hours				

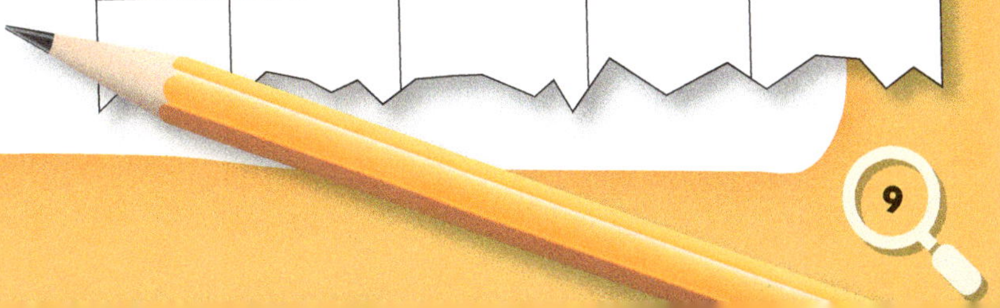

WHAT DO PLANTS NEED?

Plants need sunlight, air, water, and minerals to grow. With a good supply of all these things, a plant should grow well. If a plant does not grow well, it is probably not getting enough of at least one of them.

Indoor plants need to be watered and fed with minerals.

Soil and water

Plants are mostly made of water, so they need water to grow. They also need minerals from the soil. Indoor pot plants need plant food (with minerals) to stay healthy. Too much water can make plants rot and wilt, but without enough water, they dry out and die.

sunlight

Plants need sunlight because they use **energy** from the sun to make food in their leaves. In a rain forest, the leaves and branches of tall trees block out the sunlight. Smaller plants grow high up on the branches of the trees so that they can get enough sunlight.

Some rain forest plants grow on vines or tree trunks to help them reach the sunlight.

ACTIVITY

WATCH SEEDLINGS GROW

Geranium seedlings will work well in this activity..

You will need:

- **4 seedlings**
- **potting soil**
- **3 small flower pots**
- **small watering can**
- **jar of water**
- **ruler or tape measure**

1. Give the first seedling all it needs to grow. Plant it in soil, put it in a sunny place, and give it enough water to keep the soil moist.

2. Plant the second seedling. Keep it watered, but put it in a dark cupboard. Plant the third seedling. Put it in a sunny place, but don't water it. Put the fourth seedling in a jar of water in a sunny place.

3. Keep a record of how each seedling grows. Write your findings down on a chart.

Seedling	Day	Height	Comments
1– soil, water, sunlight	2		taller and healthy looking
	5		2 new leaves
	8		
2 – soil, water, no sunlight	2		looking a bit pale
	5		
	8		
3 – soil, no water, sunlight	2		wilting slightly

Which seedling grows the best?
Which seedling grows the worst?
What conditions do the seedlings prefer?
Why do you think that is?

You could repeat this experiment with seedlings of a different plant. Remember to wash your hands after you touch soil.

MAKING FOOD

Plants make food in their leaves. Their leaves have to be the best shape and size to catch sunlight. Broadleaf trees, such as maple and oak, have thin leaves with a large surface area to catch as much sunlight as possible.

Sunlight helps plants to make food in their leaves that gives them the energy to grow.

Photosynthesis

Photosynthesis is the way that plants make their own food. Sunlight is absorbed by the chlorophyll in their leaves. Energy from sunlight is used to turn water and **carbon dioxide** from the air into food.

Green and growing

When plants with green leaves cannot get sunlight, they start to turn yellow and droop. There is less chlorophyll in their leaves because they cannot make enough food. When the sun shines on the plant again, its chlorophyll levels rise and the leaves turn green again.

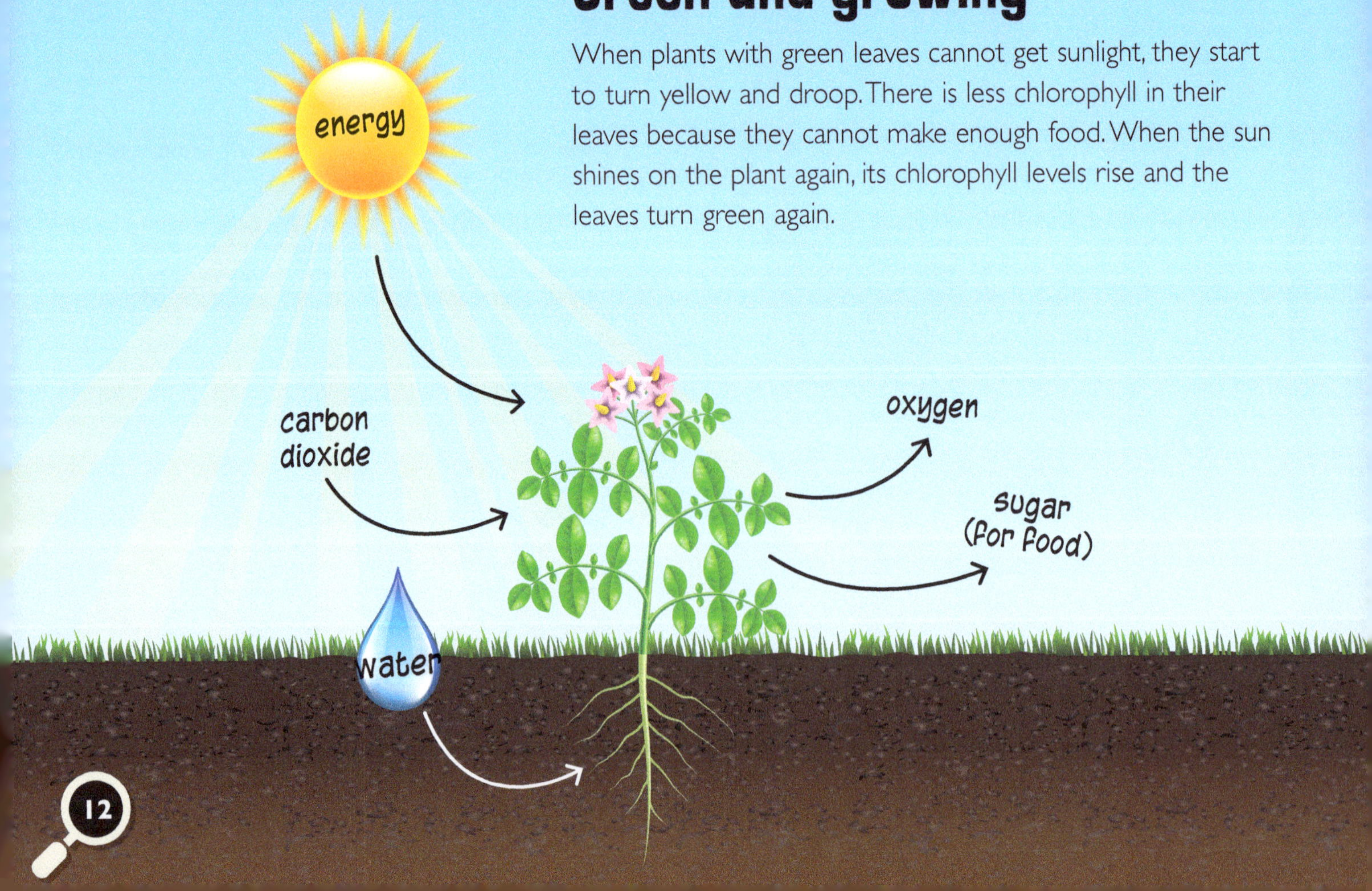

ACTIVITY

MAKE SOME LEAF STENCILS

You will need:
- **healthy houseplant with large green leaves**
- **card stock**
- **scissors**
- **sticky tack**
- **small watering can**

1. Use the card stock to cut out pairs of shapes smaller than the leaves, such as stars, diamonds, and circles.

2. Use the sticky tack to stick one shape on top of a leaf and the other directly below it on the underside of the leaf. Repeat with the other shapes on different leaves.

3. Put the plant in a sunny place and water it. After about a week, check under the shapes to see if the leaves have started to turn yellow.

How long does it take for the leaves under the card shapes to turn yellow? How long does it take for the leaves to turn green again when the card shapes are removed?

FLOWERS

Flowers contain the parts a plant needs to make seeds. Some of the seeds will grow into new plants. Seeds form after pollination has taken place.

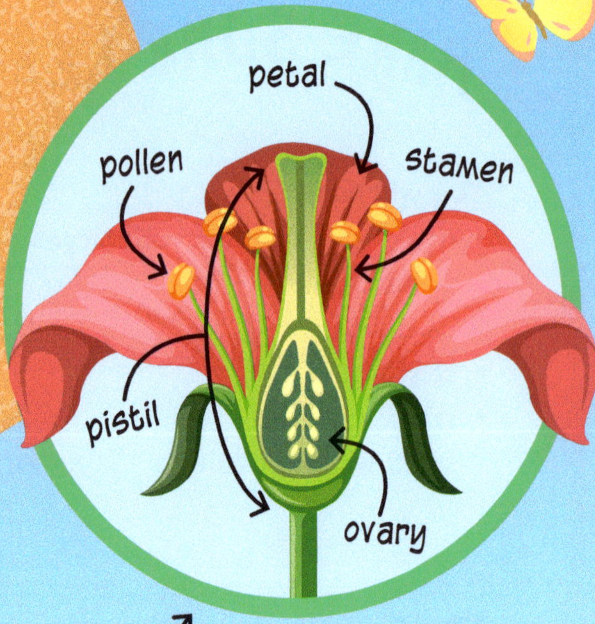

Most flowers have these parts, which are used for pollination.

Pollination

During pollination, **pollen** is carried by the wind or animals from the stamens (the male part of the flower) to the pistil (the female part). When a pollen grain reaches the **ovary**, seeds start to form. Seeds contain everything needed for a new plant to grow. Pollination usually takes place between plants. Some plants are **self-pollinated**.

Attracting insects

Some flowers have brightly colored and scented petals. They attract insects that drink a sweet juice called **nectar** from the center of the flower. As the insect drinks, pollen sticks to its legs and body. It carries the pollen on to the next flower.

ACTIVITY

DISCOVER THE PARTS OF A FLOWER

You will need:

- **big flower with colorful, scented petals**
- **white card stock**
- **clear glue or contact paper**
- **pencil or pen**

1. Carefully pull each petal off the flower. Count the petals and lay them out on the white card stock.
2. Pull off each stamen. Count them and lay them out on the card stock.
3. Remove the pistil and the ovary without separating them.
4. Write the name of the flower and label the parts.

5. Cover the whole piece of card stock with contact paperor spread glue on the card and lay the parts on top. You could also press a whole flower to include in your display.

Do this with several different types of flower. Compare the number of petals and stamens, the size and color of the petals, and anything else you notice.

GERMINATION

When a flower has done its job, it dies. Then the ovary swells and becomes the fruit that contains the seeds. The way a new plant starts to grow from a seed is called germination.

Finding seeds

Some fruits have seeds inside them. An avocado has one big seed inside it and an apple has several little seeds. Other fruits carry seeds on the outside. You can see seeds on a strawberry's skin and stripy seeds packed together on a sunflower head.

Growing seeds

Inside a seed (or a bean) is a tiny root and a shoot. The seed also has a store of food to feed the plant until it grows leaves and can make food of its own. To germinate, all seeds need water, oxygen, and the right temperature. Some seeds need darkness and others need light.

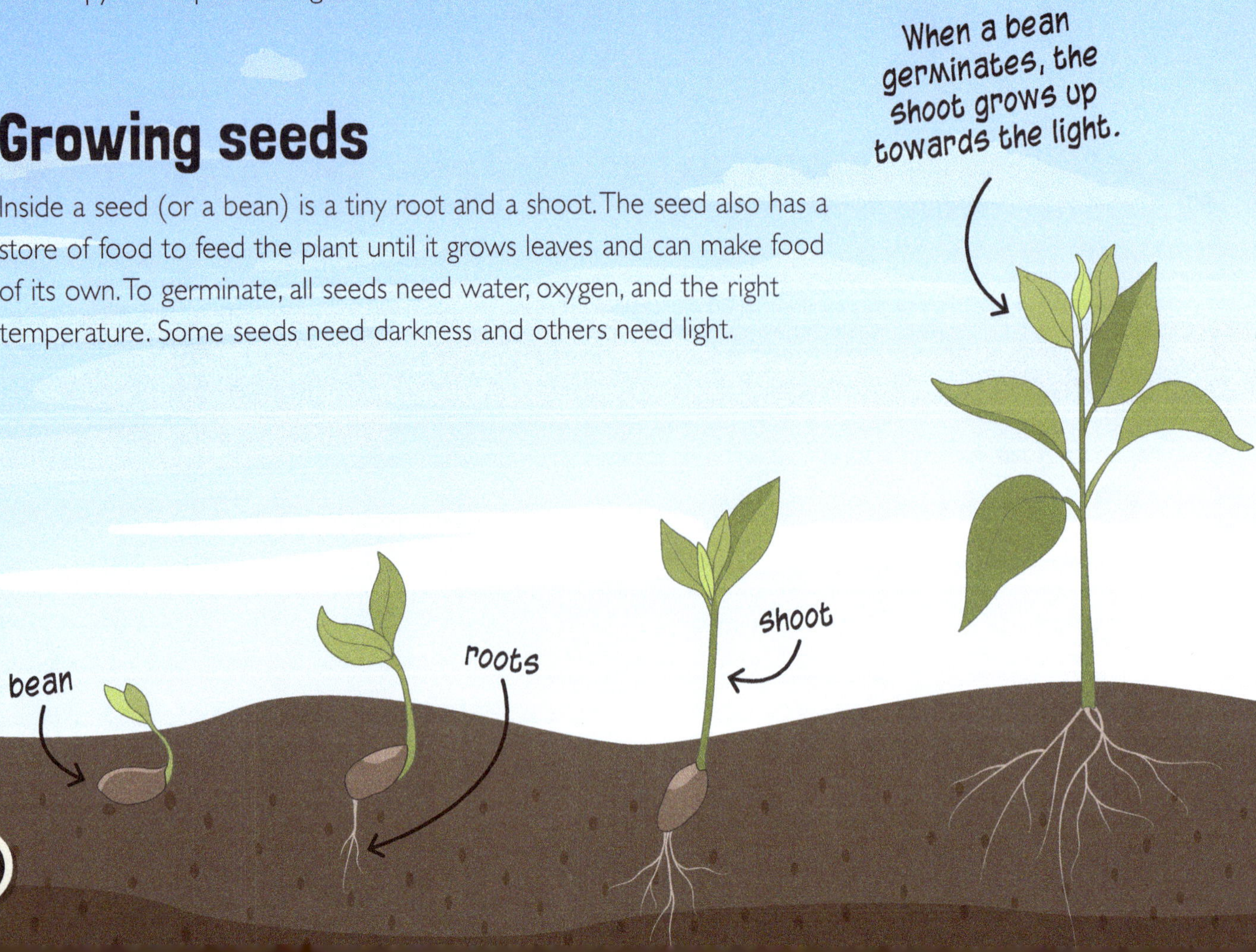

GROW BEANS IN A JAR

You will need:
- **large, flat beans such as fava beans**
- **glass jar**
- **paper towels**
- **paper**
- **ruler**
- **pencil and crayons**

1 Soak a few beans in water overnight.

2 Wet some paper towel with water. Use it to line the jar.

3 Push the beans equal distances apart in between the jar and the damp paper towel.

4 Put the jar somewhere warm and light and make sure the paper towel is always damp.

Keep a record of each new plant's growth. You could draw pictures, write comments, and take measurements. Plant the seedlings in pots of soil when they start to grow leaves.

Day	Picture of growth	Root/shoot measurements
1		0 inches
4		
7		

BULBS AND TUBERS

Some plants have **bulbs** or **tubers** that are underground food stores. Each year, a new plant grows from the bulb or tuber. The baby plant uses this store of food to grow.

A potato starts to shrivel as growing shoots use up the food it has stored.

Roots and tubers

Some plants store food, made by photosynthesis during the summer, in their roots and stems. A carrot is a root swollen with stored food and a potato is a swollen underground stem called a tuber. In the spring, shoots and new roots start to grow.

Bulbs

Onions, tulips, daffodils, and lilies are all plants that grow from bulbs. Bulbs are made up of layers of thick leaves storing food that surround a new plant waiting to grow. During the cold winter, a bulb rests under the soil. The new plant starts to grow in spring when it gets warmer.

Bulbs planted in the autumn will begin to grow in the spring.

ACTIVITY

GROW SOME NEW PLANTS

Ask an adult to help you with this activity.

You will need:

- **flower pot of soil**
- **onion**
- **carrot**
- **small plate of water**
- **4 toothpicks**
- **sweet potato**
- **jar of water**

1. Plant an onion in the flower pot, with the roots facing downward. Cover it in soil.

2. Ask an adult to slice the top off a carrot. Place the carrot top in the saucer of water.

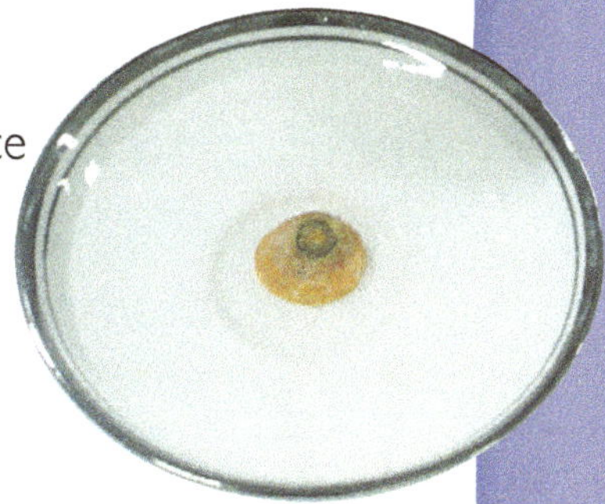

3. Push four toothpicks into the sweet potato. Use the toothpicks to hang the potato in the top of the jar so the bottom of it is in the water.

4. Keep the soil damp in the flower pot and the saucer filled with water. Make sure part of the sweet potato is always in the water.

5. Be patient over a few weeks and the bulb, the root, and the tuber will all start to grow. Keep a diary of your growing plants.

SPREADING SEEDS

Plants produce a lot of seeds because only a few seeds will find a good place to grow. Plants have many different ways of spreading their seeds to give them a good chance of starting new life.

Bright berries attract hungry birds, which help to spread the seeds.

Animals

Fruit, seeds, and nuts are all eaten by animals. When birds eat berries and fly away, the seeds later fall to the ground in their droppings. Squirrels bury nuts in the ground to eat later and then forget where some are. The "planted" nuts start to grow into new trees.

Hooks and wings

Hooks, wings, and explosions are some of the other ways that seeds spread. Seeds called hitchhikers catch onto clothes or animal fur. Maple seeds whirl through the air on wings. Cranesbill seedpods explode!

Dandelion seeds hang from parachutes that blow away in the wind.

ACTIVITY

DISCOVER SOME HIDDEN SEEDS

You will need:

- **3 seed trays**
- **trowel**
- **small watering can**
- **card stock**
- **pencil**

1. Collect soil from three different locations, such as under a sycamore tree, by a sunny wall, and next to a rose bush.

2. Put the soil in the seed trays. Label where the soil came from and the date. Water the soil lightly and keep the trays watered in a warm, light place.

3. Write down which plants were growing in each location. Write down which plants you think might grow from seeds hiding in the soil. For example, a sycamore tree because there is one nearby, or dandelions because there is uncut grass nearby.

4. When plants start to grow in the seed trays, identify them using a field guide or the internet. You could also compare them with the plants growing in each location. Were your predictions correct? Remember that some plants may look quite different when they are young.

PLANT ADAPTATION

Plants grow in different **habitats** on almost every part of planet Earth. Although all plants need sunlight, air, water, and minerals to grow, they have adapted so they can survive when any of these are in short supply.

Small plants grow on rocky mountain sides to stay sheltered from the wind.

Plant detective

Just looking at a plant can give you information about where it grows. Plants growing in dark woods often have tall stems to reach the sunlight. Mountain plants grow near the ground to protect themselves from cold winds. Desert plants store water in thick leaves or swollen stems.

Desert plants, such as these cacti, store water in their thick stems because rain is rare.

Local plants

Plants that grow naturally where you live have adapted to the local conditions. Plants brought in from other habitats may not grow so well. For example, a plant from a sunny, dry area may not grow very well in a place that is often cloudy and wet.

These plants in Italy grow well in sunny, dry conditions.

ACTIVITY

DO A LOCAL PLANT SURVEY

You will need:

- **notebook**
- **pencil and crayons**
- **camera**

Dandelion

Maple tree

Red geranium

1. Write a description of your local area and the green spaces found nearby. For example:

> A built-up town, not many gardens, a big public park nearby, a school yard with a small patch of grass, hot, dry summers and cold, snowy winters.

2. Draw a table like the one shown opposite. Take pictures (or draw sketches) of plants growing near where you live. Write where they are growing and the date you recorded them.

Plant	Location	Date
Dandelion	Front lawn	May
Maple tree	Outside our house	All year round
Red geranium	sunny porch	July

Why do you think the plants grow where you found them? Have they grown naturally or did someone plant them?

PLANTS FOR LIFE

Plants provide most of the food eaten by people all over the world every day. Eating a variety of plants can give us the goodness we need to grow and to keep strong and healthy.

In this food chain, plants make their food from sunlight, zebras eat plants, and lions eat zebras.

Food chain

A food chain shows how living things depend on each other for food. Plant-eating animals are called herbivores. Herbivores are food for meat-eating animals called carnivores. Animals who eat plants as well as meat are called omnivores.

Food plants

Most of the food you eat comes from plants or depends on plants. Bread and breakfast cereals are made from grains such as wheat, oats, and rice. Chickens that provide us with meat and eggs are fed on grain. Cows that give us meat, milk, and cheese eat grass and grains.

Farm animals eat plants to give them energy. A lot of our food depends on the energy from plants too.

ACTIVITY

DISCOVER FOOD CHAINS

You will need:

- **large sheet of paper**
- **pencils and crayons**

1. Draw a chart, like the one shown here, on the paper.

2. Write down some of the food you eat in a day in the left column. Read the ingredients on the box and look up the food in books or on the internet to trace the food chain, starting with a plant and ending with you.

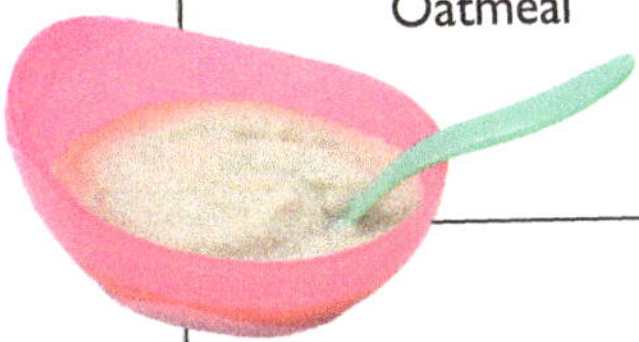

Breakfast	
Oatmeal	Oats → me
Boiled egg	Corn → chicken/egg → me
Lunch	
Cheese sandwich	Wheat/bread → me
	Grass → cow/butter → me
	Grass → cow/cheese → me
	Lettuce → me

How many food chains are you part of each day?

CARING FOR PLANTS

We need to take care of plants. They keep the planet healthy by producing oxygen. Plants also provide us with food and important medicines that help us get better when we are ill. Many of the things people do put plants at risk.

Planting trees is one way to reintroduce plants to our environment.

Deforestation

Deforestation is the cutting down of forests to clear the ground for farmland or buildings. When trees are cut down and burned, carbon dioxide is sent into the air, which traps heat from the sun. This can contribute to **global warming** and **climate change**.

What can we do?

You can help to save the world's forests by using less paper, recycled paper, or paper made from trees that will be replanted. You could also get involved in a plan to protect a local green area or start a gardening club at school.

Wood is a useful building material and used to make paper, but we need to replace the trees we cut down.

DESIGN A "CARING FOR PLANTS" PAMPHLET

What would you put in a pamplet asking people to care for plants?

For example:

Protecting plant habitats

- Buy paper and wood from forests that will be replanted.
- Support or join a local group that cleans up plant habitats, such as a local wood or a park.

Out and about

- Don't pick or uproot plants without permission.
- Watch where you walk–don't squash plants!

Growing plants

- Grow plants that attract insects needed for pollination.
- Plant a tree or sponsor a tree.

Glossary

adapt

To adapt is to change in order to survive in a particular place.

bulb

A bulb is a part of a plant that grows underground and stores food. A new plant grows from the bulb each year.

carbon dioxide

Carbon dioxide is a gas in the air that plants use to make food in their leaves.

chlorophyll

Chlorophyll is the green pigment in plants. It captures energy from sunlight to help plants grow.

climate change

Climate change is when the usual weather conditions in a place begin to change.

energy

Energy is the force that gives things the power to work. Energy gives plants the power to grow.

fruit

Fruit is the part of a plant that contains seeds.

germination

Germination is when a new plant starts to grow from a seed.

global warming

Global warming is the rise in Earth's temperature. It is partly caused by too much carbon dioxide in the air.

habitats

Habitats are the natural surroundings of plants and animals.

minerals

Minerals are chemicals found in small amounts in the soil.

nectar

Nectar is a sweet juice made by plants in their flowers.

ovary

The ovary is the part of a plant where seeds are formed.

oxygen

Oxygen is a gas in the air that animals and plants need to breathe. Animals breathe in oxygen. Plants release it.

photosynthesis

Photosynthesis is the way plants use chlorophyll, water, sunlight, and carbon dioxide to make food in their leaves.

pigment

A pigment is a natural color. Chlorophyll is the pigment that gives the stems and leaves of plants their green color.

pollen

Pollen is the yellow powder made by the male part of a plant.

pollination

Pollination takes place in a plant when a pollen grain reaches the ovary, and seeds start to form.

rain forest

A rain forest is a tropical forest of tall, broad-leaved trees in an area with high levels of rainfall.

seeds

Seeds are the parts of a plant that contain everything needed for a new plant to grow.

self-pollinated

A self-pollinated plant pollinates itself by moving pollen from its stamens to its pistil.

spores

Spores are a fine dust produced by plants that don't make seeds. A new plant grows from a spore.

tubers

Tubers are swollen roots or stems. They store food and form a new plant that grows.

water cycle

The water cycle is the way in which water moves between land, bodies of water, and the air.

water vapor

Water vapor is formed when liquid water turns into a gas.

Quiz

1. Which of the below do plants need to grow?
   a) sunlight
   b) carbon dioxide
   c) water
   d) minerals

2. Plants make food in their:
   a) roots
   b) stem
   c) flowers
   d) leaves

3. During photosynthesis, plants give off:
   a) water
   b) oxygen
   c) carbon dioxide
   d) sugar

4. What is the female part of a flower called?
   a) petal
   b) stamen
   c) pistil
   d) pollen

5. Which of the following help to carry seeds?
   a) animal fur
   b) animal droppings
   c) water
   d) wind

6. A strawberry has seeds:
   a) on the outside
   b) on the inside
   c) in the middle
   d) underneath

7. Plants growing in dark woods have:
   a) short stems
   b) tall stems
   c) thick stems
   d) thin stems

8. Which gas is released when trees are burned?
   a) carbon dioxide
   b) oxygen
   c) water vapor
   d) helium

9 **Plant-eating animals are called:**

a) carnivores
b) omnivores
c) herbivores
d) plantivores

10 **How can you care for plants?**

a) by not walking on plants
b) by watering plants
c) by planting trees
d) by using paper made from trees that will be replanted

ANSWERS 1 all of these! 2d, 3b, 4c, 5 all of these!
6a, 7b, 8a, 9c, 10 all of these!

FURTHER INFORMATION

BOOKS

A Question of Science: How can a plant eat a fly? by Anna Claybourne, Wayland

Body Bits: Eye-popping Plant Part Facts by Paul Mason, Wayland

Boom Science: Plants by Georgia Amson-Bradshaw, Franklin Watts

Outdoor Science: Plants by Sonya Newland, Wayland

WEBSITES

All about plants: www.bbc.co.uk/bitesize/topics/zy66fg8

Discover more plant facts: www.lovemyscience.com/facts-plants.html

Find out more: www.dkfindout.com/uk/animals-and-nature/plants

Index